COSMO girl!

QUIZ BOOK

DISCOVER YOUR SECRET SELF

HEARST BOOKS

A division of Sterling Publishing Co., Inc.

New York / London

www.sterlingpublishing.com

Copyright © 2008 by Hearst Communications, Inc.

Library of Congress Cataloging-in-Publication Data
CosmoGirl! quizbook : discover your secret self / the editors of CosmoGIRL!.
    p. cm.
 ISBN-13: 978-1-58816-707-1
 ISBN-10: 1-58816-707-0
1. Teenage girls--Psychology--Miscellanea. 2. Interpersonal relations in adolescence--
Miscellanea. 3. Questions and answers. I. Cosmo girl.
 HQ798.C5945 2008
 305.235'2--dc22

                          2007032053

10 9 8 7 6 5 4 3 2 1

Published by Hearst Books
A Division of Sterling Publishing Co., Inc.
387 Park Avenue South, New York, NY 10016

CosmoGIRL! and Hearst Books are trademarks of Hearst Communications, Inc.

www.cosmogirl.com

For information about custom editions, special sales, premium and corporate
purchases, please contact Sterling Special Sales Department at 800-805-5489 or
specialsales@sterlingpublishing.com.

Distributed in Canada by Sterling Publishing
c/o Canadian Manda Group, 165 Dufferin Street
Toronto, Ontario, Canada M6K 3H6

Distributed in Australia by Capricorn Link (Australia) Pty. Ltd.
P.O. Box 704, Windsor, NSW 2756 Australia

Manufactured in China

Sterling ISBN 13: 978-1-58816-707-1
        ISBN 10: 1-58816-707-0

Photo Credits:
Cover photo: Stephen Lee.
Bruno Barbazon: page 20. Stephen Lee: page 3, 4, 5, 8, 11, 16, 18, 24, 26, 28, 32, 40, 48,
54, 62, 64, 72, 78, 90. Patrick Ibanez: page 52. Christophe Meimoon: page 80, 86. David
Yellen: page 92. Thierry Van Biesen: page 36, 44, 58, 74, 84.

for fun

susan's note

Hey CosmoGIRL!s,

From working for you as your Editor-in-Chief all these years, I think probably the one thing you've told me loudest and clearest is how much you love quizzes! As you know, we publish new ones every month in the magazine *and* we put fresh ones up all the time on cosmogirl.com. But a few years ago we decided to put the best ones into a book collection, and guess what? The books *flew* off the shelves! They're in like, their *fourth* printing! So thanks for making them "best sellers," so to speak. You just can't get enough of them! (But I'm not judging you—neither can I!) Anyway, because there was such a demand for them, we decided to make a brand-new quiz book for you, filled with all the questions that help you find out more about your favorite subject: *you*! Yes, we're all a bit overly obsessed with ourselves, aren't we? But hey, who cares? Especially at this point in your life, *you* are all you really should be thinking about—who you are, who you admire, who you dream of becoming . . . It's all in good fun!

So whether you're thinking about superficial silly stuff like what sandwich you're most like, or if you're thinking about deeper stuff like what future career you might have in the White House, there's a quiz for you right here in this book. So grab your pen (if your friend wants to take it too, tell her to get her own book! Ha!) and get all quizzical on yourself. And let me know your quiz ideas whenever you have them . . . I love getting your e-mails at susan@cosmogirl.com.

Have fun, CG!s!

Love,

Susan

ARE YOU CATTY?

Find out if you're too quick to whip out your claws—or if you act more like the runt of the litter.

1. When you see a girl you know wearing the same shirt you wanted to buy, you tell her:
a. "I tried that on but I thought it looked cheap, so I put it back."
b. "I love your shirt!"—and find one like it (but better) that weekend.
c. "I was thinking of getting that, but it looks better on you, so I'm not even going to try it on now."

2. Your best friend's boyfriend has been flirting with you like crazy lately. What do you do?
a. Flirt back and then bad-mouth him to your friend.
b. Be nice to him but don't encourage or flirt back.
c. Avoid him at all costs and hope your friend doesn't find out.

3. You're hanging out with a group of people and notice that a girl you don't like has spinach in her teeth. Your next move?
a. Call it out in front of everyone, knowing it will embarrass her.
b. Keep quiet—hey, she wouldn't tell you if you had green teeth.
c. Pretend you don't see it.

4. A cute girl drops her bag and your boyfriend runs to help her pick up her stuff. You:
a. Ask her if she has her period when you see a tampon roll out.
b. Go and help them, of course.
c. Walk away; if he wants to flirt with her, there's nothing you can do about it.

TURN THE PAGE TO SEE YOUR RESULTS

5. You're playing volleyball in P.E. and your boyfriend's ex is on the other team. You make it a point to:

a. "Accidentally" nail her with a spike—right between the eyes.

b. Try your hardest not to focus on her.

c. Tell the teacher you're sick so you can sit out the game.

6. You and a friend are getting ready for a party and she asks your opinion about a not-so-flattering outfit she's trying on. You say:

a. "Totally wear it—it looks fabulous!"

b. "I'm not feeling it…what about the jeans you had on before?"

c. "You look great in everything, but that's not my favorite one."

7. You hear that a girl you know is spreading rumors about your best friend. What do you do?

a. Start spreading rumors about her. She deserves it, the little witch!

b. Find out if she really said that stuff and give your friend the full report.

c. Stay out of it—you'll just make the situation worse than it already is.

8. You're going to a party this weekend. Your crush will be there—along with another girl who likes him. When you get there, you:

a. Get them both together, then ask the girl something like, "Remember when you farted in math class on Monday? That was hilarious!"

b. Get him alone and banter with him to see whether he likes you back.

c. Let her have him—she probably has a better chance anyway.

SCORING

mostly a's: hiss!

You may not realize you're being catty but it seems like you often put other girls down to build yourself up. Even if you've been wronged in the past, remind yourself that other girls aren't always the enemy. Try to put more purr in your personality—it pays off way more than playing dirty!

mostly b's: meow!

You've got a healthy attitude toward other girls and don't see them as rivals. You know there's enough happiness to go around—so you don't sweat it if someone else is on top for a bit. Your claws do come out now and then, but it's usually when you have to defend yourself. Good kitty!

mostly c's: mew!

You're like a defenseless kitten, vulnerable to the whims of others—friends or enemies. Maybe you hold back because you're shy, but you need to fight harder for the respect you deserve. Next time, don't curl up in a ball to give others the right of way—speak up and let your thoughts be heard. Rowr!

ARE YOU A GOSSIP JUNKIE?

If gossip were a drug it'd be an out-of-control substance. Come clean and find out if you might need some rehab.

1. The best reason to have a profile on MySpace is to:
a. Keep tabs on your ex.
b. Check out photos on other people's profiles.
c. Listen to songs of new indie bands.

2. Huge news! You just found out one of the popular girls at school got liposuction. How long do you keep it to yourself?
a. Keep it? You're mass-texting people now!
b. Until someone else blabs, then you're ready to dish!
c. Forever. You don't know her so it's not your business.

3. When it comes to celebrity gossip, you:
a. Live for it—perezhilton.com is your home page!
b. Think it's entertaining—you'll flip through *US Weekly* at the nail salon.
c. They write gossip about celebs?

4. You're arriving home from spending a semester in Italy. You call your friends:
a. You texted them every day anyway!
b. After you've caught up with your family.
c. After you've unpacked and taken a long nap to fight jet lag.

TURN THE PAGE TO SEE YOUR RESULTS

5. You see the book "Why Men Have Affairs" on your friend Julie's living room table. You:

a. Tell your friends the second you leave her house!

b. Wait until you're alone and then ask Julie what's up.

c. Ignore it.

SCORING

mostly a's: bad habit

Being loaded with the latest gossip can feel empowering, but broadcasting it to the world can lead to trouble. If you keep sharing people's secrets they'll stop trusting you. Be wise: Those who talk get talked about . . and even you probably have some skeletons you want to keep in the closet!

mostly b's: mildly addicted

A little healthy dishing makes you feel connected. But while you appreciate the rush of hearing a juicy rumor, you also know when to resist the urge to spread it around. And that's good news since the gossip chain is only fun until someone—maybe even you—gets hurt.

mostly c's: squeaky clean

When it comes to gossip, you've got "earmuffs" on 24/7! But by not turning into the rumor mill, you may be missing out on what's happening around you—both good and bad. So unplug those ears and give it a whirl—it's okay to indulge every so often.

CAN YOUR FRIENDS COUNT ON YOU?

When the poo hits the fan, do you run for cover or stick around to help clean up the mess?

1. Your closest friends are most likely to call you when they need someone to help them:
a. With their guy problems.
b. Cover up the dent they put in their dad's car.
c. Throw a party.

2. Two of your friends get in a huge fight, so when one calls you to talk about it, you automatically:
a. Get the other on three-way and help them work it out.
b. Listen to her vent, but don't take sides.
c. Say, "Oh, don't worry, it'll blow over."

3. Your friend asks you to read her college application but you just don't feel like it. You:
a. Do it anyway and give her suggestions that night.
b. Do it but take a half an hour to go over it.
c. Lie and tell her you don't have time.

4. At a party, you're talking to a hot guy when you notice that your friend is stuck with a major loser. You:
a. Run right over and help her escape.
b. Rescue her if she rolls her eyes at you.
c. Keep chatting up Señor Sweetie.

5. Your friend gets bad news: Her 70-year-old aunt has died, and she's really upset. What do you do?
a. Bring over cookies you baked for her family.
b. Give her a sympathy card.
c. Leave her alone—she probably wants her space.

TURN THE PAGE TO SEE YOUR RESULTS

6. You find out that your best friend's crush actually has a thing for a girl you both hate. When do you tell your friend?

a. Right away. It's better she hears it from you.
b. You wait until she's not stressed.
c. Never! You hate giving bad news.

SCORING

mostly a's: no doubt about it!

You'd do anything for your girls and they know it! But if you're constantly all over their lives, they might feel crowded— especially those times they're not looking for help. So think before you act and ask yourself, does she need advice, or does she just need a shoulder to cry on? Your friends will love you even more!

mostly b's: that depends

Your friends line up to see you for advice. You don't like to ask your friends for help, but they know you need support once in a while (everyone does!) So ask them for help when little stress-balls hit. They'll be flattered you did and eager to return the favor.

mostly c's: don't count on it

Everyone loves your good-time-girl attitude, but since you're so busy having fun, it can be hard for your friends to rely on you. Next time you sense a friend is worried or bummed out, ask, "What's wrong?" Let her know you're there and use that wicked sense of humor of yours to help cheer her up. When you share the good times and the bad, you both win.

WHO CONTROLS YOUR LIFE?

Find out if your friends' opinions really matter or if you march to the beat of a different drum.

1. You're at a party and your favorite song comes on. No one is dancing, so you:
a. Stay put and start tapping your foot.
b. Grab your friend and make her dance with you.
c. Get up anyway and show off your latest dance moves.

2. Your curfew is an hour earlier than everyone else's. On the night of the biggest party of the school year, you:
a. Try to have as much fun as possible before going home.
b. Tell your parents it's unfair and beg them to extend it by thirty minutes.
c. Stay out the extra hour anyway and risk the consequences.

3. Your friends are obsessed with a flick you hated. When the conversation turns to the movie you say:
a. "I loved it too!"
b. "It was okay—but I've seen better."
c. "It sucked. I want those hours back!"

4. You're totally into that adorable guy in your math class, but your friends all think he's a loser. You:
a. Reconsider your crush.
b. Give it a few days to decide on your own whether he has potential
c. Think, "To each her own."

TURN THE PAGE TO SEE YOUR RESULTS

5. You might audition for the school play, but your friends don't think it's cool and try to talk you out of it. You:

a. Decide to stick to activities your friends do.

b. Persuade at least one of them to try out with you.

c. Nail your audition monologue and take the stage without them.

SCORING

mostly a's: eager to please

It's hard for you to make a move without running it past your friends. Of course you should value their opinions, but when you ignore your gut, you might be missing out on new, exciting opportunities. So don't be afraid to stand up for what you believe in—friends worth keeping will admire you all the more.

mostly b's: thorough thinker

You respect your friends' opinions—but you won't follow advice that you don't agree with. Keep on thinking things through and making the decisions that are right for you. Your friends will admire your strength and you might even inspire a few of them to branch out on their own once in a while.

mostly c's: ms. independent

You're full of self-confidence and you're not afraid to voice your opinion or try things that others might not. Stick to your guns, girl! If we all followed the crowd all the time, life would be boring. But your fierce daredevil streak leads you to amazing adventures that others might let pass them by—like the lead role in the school play!

ARE YOU A GOOD LISTENER?

Do you take it all in or let it all out? Find out if you're all ears, all mouth, or a bit of both!

1. You and your best friend just got back from being on (separate) vacations. How does the conversation go?
a. You tell every last detail of your trip.
b. You take turns telling all your fun stories.
c. She talks non-stop and you get filled in.

2. You friend calls you crying (*again!*) because her ex is dating a new girl. You're so sick of hearing about him! You:
a. Start talking about your ex to try and distract her.
b. Listen once more, but tell her she needs to move on.
c. Let her ramble on and are attentive as usual.

3. You're right in the middle of your favorite TV show when your friend calls to complain about school. What do you do?
a. Keep watching and just "uh huh" her every now and then.
b. Put the show on mute while she talks.
c. Tivo your show and give her your full attention.

4. You mom calls you with a list of things she needs you to do before you come home. You:
a. Are checking Facebook as she talks.
b. Hear the two most important tasks.
c. Write them all down as she tells you.

TURN THE PAGE TO SEE YOUR RESULTS

5. Your best friend just introduced you to her three bunk-mates from camp. Their names are:

a. Um, can I get name tags, please!

b. Jane, Sara, and you—forget the third.

c. Already stored in your brain, along with their hometowns, birthdays, and favorite bands!

SCORING

mostly a's: all mouth

You'd rather talk about yourself than listen to anyone else's problems. But acting like that shows people you don't care about your friendship, even if you do. And would you want to feel like your friends don't want to listen to your problems? No! So zip your lip every so often and give others the floor.

mostly b's: half an ear

You try to concentrate on what your friends are saying, but sometimes you find yourself making a mental to-do list or daydreaming of your latest celeb crush. Since you truly do care, try to make their conversation a priority. Turn off your cell and the TV and just listen for five minutes. You'll be glad you did—and so will they!

mostly c's: all ears

Now hear this—you're the best listener out there! When one of your friends needs to talk, she knows she can go to you and you'll be there to soak up every last word. But don't forget: Sometimes you need someone to listen to you too. Next time you're looking for advice, you can bet your friends will be more than happy to lend their ears.

ARE YOU A TEASE?

Find out if you're the kind of girl who (mercilessly!) misleads guys.

1. When you talk to a guy—whether he's just a friend or your crush—you tend to:
a. Look down or away.
b. Make eye contact.
c. Giggle a lot and make physical contact, like touching his arm.

2. When you try on outfits for big events like prom, who are you *really* hoping you'll wow?
a. Yourself.
b. Your friends.
c. Guys.

3. When your best friend's crush offers you and her a ride home after school, you:
a. Sit like a church mouse in the backseat so they can have some time alone.
b. Mention one of your best friend's accomplishments from the backseat so she looks like a superstar in front of him.
c. Blurt out "Shotgun!" and chat him up.

4. When a friend confides in you that she's totally into a certain guy, you:
a. Let her talk about him nonstop.
b. Help her come up with strategies for getting him to pay attention to her.
c. Start flirting with him, secretly hoping he'll think you're cool.

5. Do you ever bail on your friends for a guy—even one you may not be that into?
a. No way, that's not your style—guys are not *that* much of a priority.
b. It's happened once or twice, at a party or something.
c. Yup: your friends joke that they have to drag you away from guys.

TURN THE PAGE TO SEE YOUR RESULTS

6. You find out that one of your guy friends would die to date you. You don't like him like that, so:

a. You stop calling him.
b. You make sure not to hang out alone with him, and you talk about your crushes in front of him.
c. You bring him to parties and everywhere else you go, and end up grinding with him on the dance floor in front of all your friends.

7. When a guy you meet from another school asks if he can call you, you say yes, because:

a. It would be awkward to say no, and you don't want to hurt his feelings.
b. You sincerely mean it: You'd want to see him again to find out more about him.
c. You just like being thought of as the girl who guys want—even if you have no intention of dating him.

8. Would you make out with a guy who was interested in you, even if you weren't interested in him?

a. No, that's gross.
b. Maybe—he might be a good kisser!
c. You'd go for a walk but not make out.

SCORING

The letter you picked most says if you're using that back comb way too much!

mostly a's: polished pixie

You're so shy when it comes to guys that you don't even really flirt! Guys may interpret your shyness as indifference, so try to overcome your fears in small ways: Make eye contact with your crush next time, okay CG!?

mostly b's: va-va vixen

You know how to engage a guy you like in a way that makes him feel good. You also know when to hold back—you wouldn't play with a guy's mind or lead on someone who simply doesn't stand a chance with you.

mostly c's: teased-out temptress

Trying to attract every guy you meet might give you a self-esteem charge, but it could hurt a guy's feelings—and earn you a bad rep. So seek out other confidence-boosters (like hobbies) and be more selective about who you flirt with.

ARE YOU DESPERATE?

Find out if you're way too obsessed with getting a boyfriend!

1. "Big News" for you means:
a. There's been a development with a guy.
b. Your parents are making your curfew later.
c. You aced a test you were nervous about.

2. You refuse to graduate without:
a. Dating a school sports captain.
b. Cheering on your school's M.V.P. at all of his important games.
c. Breaking a school sports record.

3. How many of your friends have boyfriends?
a. All of them.
b. Some of them.
c. None of them.

4. Would you ever turn down a guy who asked you out?
a. No. I'd rather have a lame date than no date.
b. Maybe. It depends on who it was.
c. If I wasn't interested I'd let him down easy.

5. Your best friend has a hot older cousin. You:
a. Constantly bug her to set you up with him.
b. Love when she brings him up so you can talk about him.
c. Strike up a conversation with him at her birthday party.

TURN THE PAGE TO SEE YOUR RESULTS

6. Ever act wild around guys at parties?
a. Yes.
b. That depends what your definition of wild is.
c. No.

7. When an "unknown caller" shows up on your cell, you:
a. Always pick up—it could be that guy!
b. Stress, but then usually pick it up at the last minute.
c. Let it go to voicemail.

8. Would you cancel plans with a friend for a last-minute date?
a. Most likely yes.
b. Well, only if he was really cute!
c. Probably not—unless I got her blessing first.

9. You tried out for the school play because:
a. The hottest senior in school was trying out.
b. You thought it would be a fun way to meet people.
c. You love acting.

mostly a's: *muy* desperado

Trying too hard drives guys away, girl! So throw
yourself into *hobbies* you're passionate about and
you'll be too busy to worry about having a boyfriend.

mostly b's: mildly desperado

It's normal to feel lonely sometimes, but don't let the
quest for a guy consume you. Instead, when you feel
those "I don't have a boyfriend" blues coming on, have
fun with friends who make you feel special!

mostly c's: me? desperado?

Because you're not dying for guys' attention, your
confidence and independence actually end up
attracting guys to you—all the time. Ironic, no?

*Your type doesn't quite sound like you? Sometimes
we choose what we want to be, rather than what we
are. So take the quiz again with a friend who can help
you pick the most true-to-you answers!

WHAT KIND OF SEXY ARE YOU?

You have a certain something that just draws people to you! Find out what it is—and how you can use it to get the guy you want.

1. He's the first guy you've met in a while who can really make your heart jump. To let him know you're interested, you:
a. Smile and compliment his shirt.
b. Ask him what music's on his iPod.
c. Let him in on the secret move you discovered on *Halo 2*.

2. You and the guy you're into are in the same volunteer group. You love that you get to bond with him while:
a. Visiting lonely elderly people in your town.
b. Tutoring kids in math.
c. Blocking him in a super-sweaty charity basketball game.

3. You're going to a concert tonight and your crush will be there. You wouldn't leave home without:
a. A spritz of your favorite perfume—the scent just makes you feel irresistible!
b. A quirky conversation piece, like that manga book you've been reading.
c. A pair of earplugs—you'll want to get right up next to the stage for maximum noiseage.

TURN THE PAGE TO SEE YOUR RESULTS

4. Which actress would you cast to play you in a movie based on your life?

a. Jennifer Garner—you like the way she's always nice to everyone.

b. Natalie Portman—she seems to know just the right thing to say no matter what situation she's in.

c. Cameron Diaz—she's down-to-earth and not afraid to laugh at herself.

5. The cute guy in study hall has been giving you the eye almost every day. What do you do?

a. Hold his gaze a bit longer than normal, then look away coyly.

b. Write him a note that says, "Less looking, more talking. Let's get coffee!"

c. Challenge him to a staring contest—two can play at this game!

6. You're at a club when that Alicia Keys and Usher song "My Boo," starts playing. You:

a. Grab your crush and say, "Why of course you can have this dance!"

b. Ask him, "How would you like to sit out this song with me?"

c. Start fast-dancing to make him laugh, then ask him to do the robot.

7. You're talking to a cute guy at a party when he tells a "funny" story that seriously bombs. You:

a. Laugh anyway—you don't want him to be embarrassed!

b. Shake your head, smile, and say, "And it started out so promisingly!"

c. Change the subject by asking him to thumb-wrestle with you.

SCORING

Tally up your a's, b's, and c's. Then see what makes you so darn sexy!

mostly a's: you're flirty

Guys are drawn to your sweet, girly charisma and rarely feel nervous around you. But don't feel you have to hide your true feelings just to spare theirs. Guys respect a girl who's not afraid to be honest.

mostly b's: you're sharp

You radiate smart-girl charm. Guys see you as a challenge, and it makes them feel great if a girl with such high standards gives them the time of day. But let your goofy side out too— you can be the girl who's brainy *and* fun!

mostly c's: you're fun

Your no-frills nature makes you a girl and a friend rolled into one—and guys think that rocks. But show the one you like your deeper, serious side too, so he sees you as a friend who could potentially be a girlfriend.

DO YOU SCARE GUYS AWAY?

No one can read a guy's mind, but here's your chance to find out if your crush thinks you're playing it cool—or a little crazy.

1. When you start liking a guy, your philosophy is:

a. He either likes you or not—so you might as well find out now instead of wasting time wondering.

b. He'd probably like you if he got to know you— why not make a move and see?

c. There's almost no chance he'd like you because he's way out of your league, but how perfect would it be if he did?

2. At kindergarten recess, you could usually be found:

a. Chasing a boy to kiss—a new one every week.

b. Playing in the sandbox with your friends—both boys and girls.

c. Forming a girls-only club to avoid those icky boys.

3. You run into your crush and all his friends at the mall. You:

a. Yell out his name, give him a big hug and talk only to him.

b. Stop and chat with his group of friends for a few minutes, but give him a compliment so you can single him out.

c. Talk to his friends—you just can't get up the nerve to talk to him (and you'd probably say something dumb anyway).

TURN THE PAGE TO SEE YOUR RESULTS

4. You've been talking to a cute guy at school, but neither of you has made a move. Your next step:

a. Memorize his schedule and "accidentally" bump into him at least three times a day. The way you look at it, the more he sees you around, the more he'll think about you.

b. When you two are IMing, ask him to hang out with you and your friends. He seems like he's into you, so why not?

c. Hope he keeps talking to you each time you see him.

5. When you're crushing on a new guy, which animal do you channel the most?

a. A lion—bold, on the prowl, and ready to pounce.

b. A pony—you start out cautiously but get bolder once you know he likes you back.

c. An owl—super-mysterious and hard for other people to read.

6. When do you start calling a guy your boyfriend?

a. After dating for about a week—what's the big deal?

b. After a month or so— you don't want to seem too excited.

c. Only after he calls you the g-word first.

7. The first time you meet a guy's parents, you:

a. Beg to see naked baby pictures of their adorable son.

b. Ask the usual small-talk questions about their family to get the conversation going.

c. Usually muster only one-word answers to all their questions. The whole experience is so awkward!

mostly a's: run!

You think, I like him, so why shouldn't I go for it? Being strong-willed can be hot, but when it's too obvious you're into him—and you create ways to be with him rather than let them happen—you could weird him out. You may also look desperate (even if you're not). So curb your enthusiasm a bit—subtlety can pay off!

mostly b's: sweet!

You flirt, but you're not one to assume he's interested before he's given you some signs. Guys respond to your steady strategy because they get a chance to warm up to you at their own pace, and you're comfortable taking it slow too. Plus, they see you as a bit of a mystery, which they can't help but want to solve.

mostly c's: who's she?

Being a lovezilla isn't your nature, but if you don't send any signals that you're into him, he'll never know! Your crush needs a bit of encouragement, since guys are just as scared of rejection as you are. (And sometimes they're just plain oblivious!) Start small: One little smile won't make him think you're in love with him. But it could cause a spark!

ARE YOU WRECKING YOUR LOVE LIFE?

Find out if you're building a good foundation for longterm love—or demolishing your chances at romance!

1. New school year, clean slate for love! What's your romance goal for the coming year?

a. To find a cute new boyfriend ASAP!

b. To find your soul mate.

c. To kiss as many hotties as possible! You only live once, right?

d. To have a fun dating life but not ever get your heart broken.

2. You're waiting for your friend to finish buying something at the mall when a cute salesguy strikes up a conversation with you. You:

a. Give him your secret "boyfriend potential" test. If he passes, you'll ask him to grab a bite with you and your friend on his break.

b. Decide he's not your type if he's a guy who goes up to girls at malls.

c. Flirt until he asks for your number. One more for your little black RAZR!

d. Chat a little to see if he's cool.

3. The last time one of your relationships ended, how did you deal?

a. You moved right into a new relationship. It's the best way you know of to get over someone.

b. It took a while for you to move on. You kept always comparing guys to your ex and finding things wrong with them.

c. Relationship? You haven't been with someone long enough to actually go through a breakup!

d. You wallowed for a week and then forced yourself to get back out there.

TURN THE PAGE TO SEE YOUR RESULTS

4. A friend wants to set you up with her hot cousin. So you:

a. Say, "Sure! When?" before she even finishes her sentence.

b. Stalk his MySpace to see if you're into the same bands and stuff. If his tastes are different, it's a no-go.

c. Ask her to invite him to a party this weekend so if you're not into him, you can flirt with the other guys there.

d. Just let things play out naturally. You might see him at a basketball game next week. If sparks fly, then great.

5. Which celeb's love life is most like yours?

a. Mandy Moore. She moves seamlessly from one serious relationship to the next.

b. Natalie Portman. She'd rather be single than casually date someone she's only sort of into.

c. Lindsay Lohan. She has a ton of prospects and loves getting the eye of every guy in the room.

d. Keira Knightley. She knows love when she sees it and isn't afraid to commit when it's there.

SCORING

mostly a's: you're a serial dater

It seems like you're always in a relationship with barely any time off in between. Yeah, it feels good to be part of a couple, but make sure you're with a guy because you like him, not because you don't like to be alone.

mostly b's: you're overly picky

It's good to have high standards, but don't be so quick to shut out guys who aren't your "type." Try to open yourself up to connecting with guys who don't fit your first-glance criteria. You may find one who really "gets" you after all!

mostly c's: you're boy-crazy

Flirting with tons of guys is fun, but when you do take the time to get a feel for what it's like to connect with just one guy, you'll be part of a couple. And that can be just as much fun as playing the field.

mostly d's: you're in control

Your thinking is right on target. If love presents itself, you know how to recognize it and go for it. And if it doesn't, you have fun anyway. That open-minded attitude will lead you to a solid romantic future (no bulldozers in sight!).

DO YOUR BOYFRIEND'S FRIENDS LIKE YOU?

Are you an innie or an outie? Discover your status within his group of friends.

1. When you interrupt your boyfriend and his buddies watching *Kung Fu Hustle*, they:

a. Turn up the volume and pretend they don't see you.

b. Mumble, "Hey," without looking away from the screen.

c. Offer you a spot on the sofa and a playful karate chop.

2. Your boyfriend is out of town and his best friend is throwing a party. Do you go?

a. No way. You weren't even invited—as if you care.

b. Of course! You're in charge of the late-night snacks!

c. Probably. His friends won't stop texting you to "Be there!"

3. You're stuck in a car with your boyfriend and his crew. Where do you sit?

a. In the driver's seat. You don't trust them at the wheel.

b. The middle backseat, so you're at the center of 'em all.

c. Shotgun! They really know how to treat a lady.

4. When you're giving your guy the silent treatment, his friends:

a. Take him out to meet other girls.

b. Play peacemaker—there's too much testosterone in the group without you around!

c. Say, "It sucks that you two are on the outs," then let you know they're available if you want to talk.

TURN THE PAGE TO SEE YOUR RESULTS

4. Which show's title best describes your relationship with your boyfriend's bunch?

a. Dirt.
b. My Boys.
c. Entourage.

SCORING

mostly a's: no love lost

You and your guy's gang just don't mix. While that tension can be tricky for your boyfriend, there's no law that says you have to love his friends. As long as you let him have quality time with them sometimes, you can all share him!

mostly b's: but of course!

To your boyfriend's buds, you're more than just his girlfriend—you're their BFF too! But don't start scratching your junk in front of them—there's nothing cooler than a girl who can hang out with the boys without actually becoming one of them.

mostly c's: a little too much . . .

Aw! After spending time with you, the guys really like you—like, *like you* like you. But don't worry. When a guy's friends dig his girl, it only makes her that much more special to him. Just be very careful not to flirt with them—you're a one-guy girl!

WHAT'S YOUR KISSING I.Q.?

Time to enroll in Kissing U! Find out if you'll be an incoming freshman or P.h.D. candidate.

1. What's your idea of the perfect first-date kiss?

a. "Kisses" plural is more like it!

b. A sneak-attack smooch.

c. A sweet good-bye peck.

2. Have you ever practiced kissing on the back of your hand?

a. Yes. Practice makes perfect, right?

b. A couple of times, but not anymore.

c. Maybe once or twice, but I'd never tell anyone that!

3. What are you wearing on your lips right now?

a. Cinnamon-flavored lip plumper.

b. Shimmery lip gloss.

c. ChapStick.

4. What's the one thing you can't go without on a date?

a. Brown-sugar lip scrub— soft lips are sexy lips!

b. Peppermint Altoids—it's all about the breath!

c. Your best friend—double dates are more fun and less stressful.

5. Over-the-top, super-steamy love scenes in movies make you:

a. Swoon! You live for passion!

b. Warm and fuzzy. Especially ones with Jude Law!

c. Blush. Time for another popcorn refill!

TURN THE PAGE TO SEE YOUR RESULTS

SCORING

---

mostly a's: phi beta kisser!

When it comes to kissing, you're at the head of the class! Your kissing M.O. is simple: Smooch well and smooch often, even if it's on your first date with a guy! As long as you keep things from getting too heated up, why not have a little fun?

mostly b's: lip smacker

Although you love to pucker up, you make a guy work for it! Sometimes this means you'll lock lips on the first date, sometimes not until the fifth. You wait until it feels right and when it is (whether it's sooner or later) the guy who gets to smooch you knows he's pretty special!

mostly c's: smart smoocher

To you, kissing is so intimate that the thought of it freaks you out a bit. But don't worry—if you're a snogging rookie, it'll just take time (and a sweet someone to practice with) before you're bumped up to the big leagues!

ARE YOU BITTER ABOUT LOVE?

Roses are red, violets are blue. Do you spread the love, or want to squash it with the bottom of your shoe?

1. Your school is selling roses for Valentine's Day. You order:

a. A dozen—all for your sweetie or crush.

b. One for each of your best friends.

c. None. That tradition is dumb.

2. Tomorrow is the 14th of February. You'll most likely be wearing:

a. A pink shirt, of course!

b. Whatever you pull out of your closet, but you accessorize with a heart locket.

c. All black, in mourning!

3. Okay, last V-day question, we swear! When you remember that Valentine's Day is coming up, you:

a. Are psyched—you love the holiday!

b. Don't obsess, but you do love those candy hearts!

c. Gag (What?! It's a reflex!)

4. You meet a cute, funny guy at a party and exchange numbers (score!), but he reminds you of your ex (sigh). When he texts you, you:

a. Arrange to hang out right away—new guy, new start!

b. Write him back and take your chances.

c. Ignore his message—what's the point, it'll never work.

TURN THE PAGE TO SEE YOUR RESULTS

5. When you pass the guy you like in the hall, your usual M.O. is to:
a. Run over and start chatting him up.
b. Smile and say hi.
c. Look straight ahead.

6. When was the last time you were really, really into a guy!
a. Right now. Actually you always are!
b. When you were dating your ex last year.
c. Not since you were 11!

7. You're going out with a guy for the first time. What's your plan?
a. Rent your favorite romantic movie.
b. Go bowling. It's kitschy and fun.
c. Who cares—you'll inevitably breakup.

mostly a's: sugar-coated

You see the world through candy-colored glasses. You're always open to love, but if you give it away too easily, there's a chance you may get hurt. Just be sure those you shower with love and affection do the same for you. Otherwise, keep being your sweet self!

mostly b's: semisweet

You appreciate love and romance but realize it's not the answer to everything. That optimistic—but not overly obsessed—attitude helps you attract guys and it makes you open to relationships without feeling the need to listen to sappy love songs on repeat or bake pink cookies for your homeroom!

mostly c's: bitter, much?

Your down-with-love vibes could block you from connecting with someone cool. Even if things went sour with guys in the past, it won't always be that way so don't shut them down before giving each new cutie a chance. Let your love life get a sugar rush at least once in a while and who knows, you might eventually end up with a sweet tooth!

WHERE WILL YOU MEET YOUR NEXT BOYFRIEND?

Find out where he's hanging out and go get him this weekend!

1. In the movie of your life, who would you cast as your leading man?
a. Shy James Franco.
b. Athletic Channing Tatum.
c. Intelligent Jake Gyllenhaal.
d. Cool Adrian Grenier.

2. For your next birthday, you definitely want to get:
a. A new laptop.
b. Portable speakers for your iPod.
c. An iPhone.
d. A vintage U2 tee.

3. What's your perfect dream date?
a. A romantic beach picnic.
b. Going insane at a Lakers game.
c. Browsing a new exhibit at a museum.
d. Being serenaded at an open-mic night.

4. It's Friday night, time to have fun! Where are you?
a. Watching "Grey's Anatomy."
b. Playing laser tag with your friends.
c. Checking out a foreign flick with subtitles.
d. Flirting with the cute waiter at a coffee shop.

5. Which of these activities are you most likely to join at school?
a. Lit mag.
b. Varsity tennis.
c. Debate team.
d. Stage crew.

TURN THE PAGE TO SEE YOUR RESULTS

SCORING

mostly a's: on facebook

You're witty and introspective, but sometimes a little on the shy side. You like chatting online before you meet someone face-to-face. Send a message to the guy you friended last week and arrange a group date with all your pals. Before you know it, you may soon switch your status from "Single" to "In a Relationship."

mostly b's: at a sporting event

You're a bundle of energy and so outgoing that you seem to attract friends anywhere. Whether you're scoring the winning point for your team or just on the sidelines supporting your fellow athletes, everyone is routing for you (or with you!). So you're bound to find your love at the next big game . . . or he'll find you!

mostly c's: in class

You're so smart that you're always looking for interesting new ways to challenge your mind. Try putting your head together with the cutie in your class who may need help with a test coming up. Suggest a cozy cram session for two—and then be sure to take a few study breaks (wink!).

mostly d's: at a concert

From scouring thrift stores for vintage finds to filling your MP3 player with the latest indie groups, you're into doing your own thing. So when you're checking out that band you love, look around: There's a one-of-a-kind guy in the crowd who's ready to groove to your unique beat.

*Your type doesn't quite sound like you? Sometimes we choose what we want to be, rather than what we are. So take the quiz again with a friend who can help you pick the most true-to-you answers!

WHICH PAIR OF JEANS MATCHES YOUR PERSONALITY?

Like a tried and true friend, jeans will never let you down. Take this quiz to find out which pair is your perfect fit!

1. It's your friend's birthday. What do you get her?
a. Flowers, balloons, and a card.
b. You'll make her something special.
c. A chic pair of aviators.

2. If money were no object you'd show up to prom in:
a. A 1969 Mustang convertible.
b. A Toyota Prius hybrid.
c. A silver BMW M3.

3. Time for spring break! Where do you dream of spending the week?
a. Island hopping on a Caribbean cruise.
b. Exploring modern art galleries in New York City.
c. Scoping out the hottest boutiques in Paris.

4. What are you most looking forward to the about going to college?
a. Being on your own, finally!
b. Having your own place to decorate.
c. Taking cool classes.

5. Your hair is usually:
a. Pulled back in a neat ponytail.
b. In some funky cut or style—you like to stand out from the crowd.
c. Flat ironed and sleek.

6. If you could bring along a celebrity pal to go shopping with you, it would be:
a. Reese Witherspoon.
b. Gwen Stefani.
c. Victoria "Posh" Beckham.

TURN THE PAGE TO SEE YOUR RESULTS

SCORING

mostly a's: boot-cut jeans

You're a classic, just like a good pair of boot-cut jeans. Whether you're dressed up or going casual, you exude an easy-going, relaxed attitude. Your down-to-earth nature makes people feel comfortable and your friends flock to you for advice and support.

mostly b's: customized jeans

You are a free spirit. No way would you conform to anyone's rules, and you've got the look to prove it. Whether you're embellishing your jeans with rhinestones, bleaching them out, or cutting them all up, you add your unique take on life to whatever you wear!

mostly c's: skinny jeans

Like a great pair of skinny-jeans, you are sophisticated and chic. Always one step ahead of the trends, people look to you for your sense of style. And you love to show it off—life is one big catwalk and every chance you get, you strut your stuff!

WHAT'S YOUR SECRET POWER?

You've got a hidden talent. Find it—and we'll tell you how to make money off it. Deal?

1. You're in a "good guys vs. bad guys" movie. Which good-guy role would you choose to play?
a. An FBI agent. You love to dissect clues and save the day!
b. An international spy. You'd do your own stunts, thankyouverymuch.
c. A cop (with a heart of gold!). Your gut always leads you to the truth.
d. A prosecutor. You'll make the bad guys play by the rules.

2. If your crush gave you a compliment (and why not? You deserve it!), which one would you be most likely to get?
a. "You're hot, and it's awesome that you're so smart too."
b. "You're hot, and I always have so much fun with you."
c. "You're hot, and you really get me better than anyone else."
d. "You're hot, and you give me the best advice."

3. Okay, admit it (we won't tell a soul!). What's your secret cable-channel addiction?
a. The Discovery Channel.
b. The Sci-Fi Channel.
c. A&E (love the Biography series!).
d. Lifetime Television.

TURN THE PAGE TO SEE YOUR RESULTS

4. At your best friend's party, you're likely to be:
a. Playing a game.
b. Dancing like a wild woman.
c. Having an intense conversation with just a few people.
d. Making yummy hors d'oeuvres.

5. You're doing a group project at school. You:
a. Volunteer to research it. You love surfing the Web.
b. Come up with really creative ways to present the topic to the class.
c. Know who's going to butt heads in the group, and play peacemaker.
d. End up doing most of the work since everyone else usually slacks off!

6. If there's one thing you can't stand, it's when you feel:
a. Like you look dumb.
b. Caged up like a zoo animal.
c. Betrayed by someone you love.
d. As useless as navel lint.

7. Your crush mumbles a message on your answering machine, and you can't understand him. You:
a. Play back the tape over and over and carefully consider the different reasons he might have called.
b. Call him back to find out what he wanted. What've you got to lose?
c. Call your friends and analyze why he might have called you.
d. Think his mumbling means he's nervous around you… which can only signify that he really, really likes you!

SCORING

secret strength: intellect

words to describe you: logical, strong-willed, innovative

power profile: You know that saying, "knowledge is power"? You're a sharp thinker, and your emotions don't get in the way of your decision making. You like to reflect on any experience to see what you can take away from it—whether it's good or bad. You think, "Okay, what did I learn and how can I use it in the future?" The result? Since you hate passing up opportunities, you tend to overload yourself and get stressed out. But your need to be in control whips you back on track.

how to work it: You're always thinking so fast that before you can put one idea into action, you've moved on to the next one. Make those ideas into success stories by strategizing! First, get yourself a special dream book, where you can jot down your interests and ideas. Soon you'll start to see that a basic interest in, let's say, travel, might morph into an idea for a teen travel guide. Whatever it is, it jumps out and says, "Pick me! You can do this!" Next: Own your idea. Plot out the steps to making it real (ask a teacher to help you write a book proposal, talk to a travel agent about getting free trips for research), and get started! That little book idea might get you a publishing deal and nationwide tour! Now, maybe you don't want to write a book. Fine—it's up to you to figure out what you'll do to make that dough. But if you follow this advice, it's only a matter of time before you will!

mostly b's: you're a free spirit

secret strength: open-mindedness

words to describe you: unconventional, daring, optimistic

power profile: Some might call you a rebel, but you prefer "nonconformist." If the world didn't have people with "it's so crazy it might just work!" ideas like you do, there's no way we'd have cell phones, planes, or Napster. (Thanks!) But since spontaneity is your way of life, you tend to be a tad disorganized (just a tad!). Still, you're a charmer who everyone loves being around and who's known for turning even the most boring situation into a total blast.

how to work it: You can't just wing it when it comes to real success. The trick to making your multimillion-dollar ideas into real multimillions is the follow-through. So rally your entourage (you know, the people who'll be able to say they knew you when), and ask them to stay on your back about that goal you want to go after— whether it's Hollywood stardom or the dog-walking charity fashion show you dreamed up. Get a friend to help you create an action plan, ask another friend for her input, and so on. The more people who see you're serious about meeting this goal, the more people who will ask you if you've made any progress. You won't want to let them down, so you'll be motivated to keep at it. The bottom line? Marry your risk-taking ability with stick-to-it-iveness, because as the saying goes, "genius is 1 percent inspiration and 99 percent perspiration." If you follow through, there's no telling how much money you'll rake in. Um, can we have your autograph now?

mostly c's: you're a visionary

secret strength: intuition

words to describe you: idealistic, sensitive, articulate

power profile: You're the ultimate people person. With your excellent listening skills, you "hear" what people aren't saying as well as what they are saying. (Psst! Your gut tells you!) Because you divide your energy among lots of people (you've got tons of friends), you sometimes end up putting your own goals on the back burner. Still, when you do dream, you dream big because you not only see what is, but what could be and what should be. It's a rare skill to have!

how to work it: How many times have you ignored your instincts and listened to someone else's advice? And how many times have you thought, "I should've gone with my gut!" Let that be your mantra, girlfriend. Use that amazing intuition to let your own personal truth lead you to your success. The next time you've got some life dilemma and friends give you their input, go spend time alone to reconnect with yourself. Write down everyone else's thoughts so you have them (after all, their advice doesn't always suck). Then pretend a friend came to you with this same problem. What would you tell her? That first reaction is what you should follow—even if you have to go against the grain. Whether you want to start your own magazine, direct a film, or do anything that makes someone ask, "How are you ever going to do that?" just know you'll find a way. People in high places will be impressed with your faith in yourself and put a nice paycheck behind it!

mostly d's: you're a guardian angel

secret strength: maturity

words to describe you: responsible, supportive, organized

power profile: Okay, were you born grown up? You're the "put-together" girl who always keeps her head. So it's no wonder that you often find yourself being the plan maker! But by always taking charge, you sometimes end up resenting other people for slacking. Still, you really do love the fact that others feel safe with you around. Taking care of people makes you feel good.

how to work it: First, you've got to learn to let some things go. You don't have to be the one who does everything. But when something is really important to you—say, the planning of the prom—the key is to share the load. It's called delegating, and it's about you being the boss (like the sound of that?) and relying on others to do the individual tasks. By stepping back from the grunt work, you're in a position to make sure everything happens according to your very smart plan. The hard part is giving people orders in a way that doesn't make them feel like they're being bossed around. So instead of saying, "You should do blah-blah," try, "I'm thinking you'd be great at blah-blah!" Then, trust them to come through for you. If you give people stuff they'll be good at, you'll find they're psyched to pitch in. Once you master the skill of harnessing people-power, you'll meet your goals—and today and in the future!—much more quickly. And since managing people isn't easy, when you're a pro at it, you'll hear—"Okay, how much do you want to be paid?" *Cha-ching!*

ARE YOU PARANOID?

Find out if you have a tendency to freak out for no freakin' reason!

1. You're taking a biology test that's graded on a curve. You:

a. Tilt your desk away from everyone and write super-small.

b. Keep your answer covered with your arm.

c. Think, Who'd ever cheat off of me? Cheaters never win!

2. New semester, new locker combo. Where's the tape it was on?

a. Torn up and thrown in separate trash cans.

b. Somewhere hidden safely at home.

c. Tucked in the back of your daily planner.

6. You're walking home at night and hear steps behind you. You:

a. Run like hell.

b. Glance around to see who it might be.

c. Don't even break a sweat.

4. At the mall, you could swear people keep checking out your butt. You assume:

a. You have a big period stain on your tush.

b. That they must be looking at your cool shopping bag from that new store.

c. They're admiring your hot new pants.

5. Some guy comes up to you on the street and says, "Hey, aren't you a model?" You think:

a. Nice line, Bozo.

b. Wow! Your new haircut must look great!

c. Omigosh! How sweet!

6. When your teammates say, "Great job!" after the game, you think:

a. I must usually *really* suck.

b. I know I can do even better next time.

c. It's cool they're happy for me.

TURN THE PAGE TO SEE YOUR RESULTS

7. You get a voice mail saying, "Call back to claim your free trip to the tropics!" You think:

a. "Pshh—scam city."
b. "Too bad it's probably not real. A free trip would have rocked!"
c. "Cool! Free vacation!"

8. Your boyfriend seems quiet. He must:

a. Be mad at you.
b. Have something on his mind.
c. Not feel like talking.

SCORING

mostly a's: completely paranoid

Chill, sister! Full-blown panic attacks regularly = bad. Everyone is *not* out to get you . . . or are they? Just kidding. They're not. We promise!

mostly b's: wisely skeptical

Your inquiring mind could be onto something. You look at all the facts and make realistic conclusions. Next stop: *CSI: Miami*!

mostly c's: totally unsuspecting

Here on Earth, everything is not always as it appears. Watch faces, actions, and body language to get the real story.

WHAT DOES YOUR BEDROOM SAY ABOUT YOU?

Discover how your clutter can be a clue to your personality.

1. What does your bed look like on an average day?
a. Like it was devoured by your wardrobe.
b. Unmade with a few things on it.
c. Neatly made with pillows fluffed.

2. Quick! Where is your favorite pair of jeans?
a. In your room, flung over a chair or a lamp or something.
b. On the floor of your closet where you left them.
c. Neatly folded in your jeans drawer.

3. When was the last time you could see your floor?
a. Wait!? My room has a floor?
b. A few days ago.
c. You're looking at it now.

4. Your shoes are organized in your closet by:
a. Whatever direction you threw them in.
b. Season.
c. Color, season, and heel height.

5. Your new guy is coming over in five minutes. What do you need to do to get your room boyfriend-ready?
a. Hope for a miracle!
b. Make your bed, hang up some clothes, and straighten your desk.
c. Open the door for him

TURN THE PAGE TO SEE YOUR RESULTS

SCORING

mostly a's: miss messy

You're laid-back and easygoing—and it shows. You'll clean when you absolutely have to, like when the laundry on the floor prevents you from opening your bedroom door! Your mess may drive your parents up the wall but it doesn't bother you one bit—you prefer your room to match your ultra-relaxed personality!

mostly b's: organized chaos

You've got your own system worked out—you know where everything is, even if no one else does! Having some order gives you peace of mind, so you'll straighten up when it gets too insane but you don't have time to go overboard—there are plenty of more important (i.e: fun!) things you can be doing besides cleaning.

mostly c's: neat freak

Admit it—you have to stop yourself from cleaning when you're over at a friend's house! You're efficient and live by the motto, "a place for everything and everything in its place." Your room reflects this and being clutter-free is your key to staying in control—there's nothing worse to you than wasting time digging around in a mess!

WHAT KIND OF SANDWICH ARE YOU?

Everyone's hungry to meet someone new—but how appetizing are your ingredients?

1. If your life were a movie, it would be:
a. A romantic comedy.
b. A sub-titled drama.
c. An action-packed suspense.

2. Your perfect date outfit is:
a. A cute top and jeans—you feel sexy when you're comfy.
b. A new mini-dress—you love to wear something chic and flirty.
c. Lots of layers—you never know how you'll feel.

3. What does your usual weekend consist of?
a. Fri. with friends, Sat. with your guy, Sun. homework.
b. Divided between friends, family, and a little alone time.
c. Usual? Never! You're always doing something new.

4. It's your birthday! What's your ideal way to celebrate?
a. The basics: cake, dinner, a few close friends.
b. A party with tons of interesting, new people!
c. A trip to a place you've never been!

5. The best way to get a hold of you:
a. Just show up at your house!
b. Call your cell—you always pick up.
c. Send a text—you'll write back when you get a sec.

TURN THE PAGE TO SEE YOUR RESULTS

SCORING

mostly a's: the open-faced turkey melt

Like this yummy dish, what you see is what you get! You lay all of your feelings out on the table: If you're having a bad day, everyone knows it; if you like someone, you always let them know it. Being straightforward is great at times, but it may help your game to switch it up a bit and leave some things to the imagination.

mostly b's: the grilled panini

Your close friends know the real you, but when it comes to meeting new people you like to make them work for it! You've got an allure that keeps them wanting more and like this European 'wich, you're a bit sophisticated with just the right amount of layers to keep people guessing. Delish!

mostly c's: the monster club with everything on it

You've got so much going on in your head, people are never quite sure what might be inside—just like with this mega-meal! You're edgy and fun, always up for an adventure, and you love to keep everyone on their toes. A little mystery never hurt anyone, but sometimes it makes it hard for people to see the true you. So open up and let 'em know what it is you're thinking every once in a while!

WHAT'S YOUR MUSICAL MOVIE MATCH?

Admit it! You love to sing in the shower and dance around when you're alone. Give into your guilty pleasure and see what big-screen musical you're meant to star in!

1. You're channel surfing after school, what catches your eye?
a. A dramatic/sappy Lifetime Original Movie.
b. A silly show on Comedy Central.
c. A steamy daytime soap.

2. What old-fashioned era had the best style?
a. 1950s—it was all about ladylike glamour.
b. 1960s—clothes were fun, colorful, and crazy.
c. 1920s—women dressed sexy but sophisticated.

3. Oh, man! There's an awful rumor about you going around school. How do you deal?
a. Write down your feelings in your journal.
b. Laugh it off—it's so obviously not true.
c. Start your own spicy rumor.

4. Your MySpace profile has tons of:
a. Meaningful quotes and lyrics.
b. Hilarious pictures of you and your friends.
c. Flirty messages from hot guys.

5. The best way to get your crush's attention is to:
a. Leave him a sweet love note.
b. Crack a joke that makes him laugh.
c. Lock eyes and subtly smile when you pass him in the hall.

TURN THE PAGE TO SEE YOUR RESULTS

mostly a's: *Dreamgirls*

You're a romantic who is always daydreaming about how your life might turn out. Sometimes you can get lost in your own fantasies and just like Miss Effie White, it's your hopeful outlook on life that will help you dust yourself off when things get tough, and carry you on to sparkling success!

mostly b's: *Hairspray*

Like perky and positive Tracy Turnblad, you can be a little goofy sometimes. But people are drawn to your sunny, upbeat personality. Although you may act all fun and games, deep down you know you were meant to somehow make a difference in the world and always have an agenda ready to help get what you want!

mostly c's: *Chicago*

You love that people (especially guys) find you a little mysterious. There's an inner vixen inside you that would make Roxie Hart proud, but people have to know you really well to discover her! They'll have to break through your many intriguing layers, but once they meet your fun and flirty side, they'll find it was worth the time.

WHAT'S YOUR ROMANTIC MOVIE METER?

Take our trivia quiz to see if mushy movies make you cry tears of joy—or pain!

1. In *The Notebook*, how many letters does Noah write Allie?
a. 365, one every day for a year.
b. 364, once a week for seven years.
c. One, and then he stops when she doesn't reply.

2. In *Love, Actually*, where does the movie start and end?
a. Heathrow airport.
b. The Prime Minister's house.
c. Notting Hill.

3. In *High School Musical 2*, what does Troy give to Gabriella on the last day of school?
a. A necklace with a "T" for Troy.
b. His yearbook to sign.
c. The lyrics to a new song.

4. In *Enchanted*, who pushes Princess Giselle down the well?
a. Prince Edward's step-mother
b. The dragon.
c. One of the seven dwarves.

5. In *Titanic*, where are Rose and Jack when they first kiss?
a. At the front of the ship pretending to fly.
b. Dancing below deck.
c. Exploring the luggage room.

6. In *Grease*, what sport does Danny get a letter in to impress Sandy?
a. Track.
b. Wrestling.
c. Car racing.

TURN THE PAGE TO SEE YOUR RESULTS

SCORING

mostly a's: grab the tissues!

You're a chick flick champ! You feel the love (and heartbreak!) of romantic movies as if it's all really happening to you! Just keep those Kleenex nearby to dry your tears—and remember to take five from movies every once in a while and go create your own happily ever after!

mostly b's: fast-forward to the good stuff!

You might not remember every line, but you love that warm and fuzzy feeling you get from watching a good romantic flick whether it's with your latest crush or just your best girl friends. Comfy couch, junk food, on-screen Prince Charming—that's your idea of a perfect Friday night!

mostly c's: pass the popcorn!

Who needs fantasy romance when you can have the real thing?! You're much more into the cutie that's sitting next to you than the movie on the screen. You think that, locking lips with the leading guy in your life is way more appealing than an over-the-top movie kiss any day!

ARE YOU HIGH MAINTENANCE?

When it comes to your beauty regimen, are you a prima donna…or a natural woman?

1. You have a big date tonight—and an even bigger zit. What do you do?
a. Reschedule and hide in your house until it's gone!
b. Cover it up with tons of concealer.
c. Relax—you doubt he'll even notice.

2. When was the last time you got your nails done?
a. The polish is drying as you take this quiz.
b. Less than a month ago.
c. For a special occasion, like prom.

3. Visualize all the makeup products you own. What kind of bag would you need to fit your entire stash?
a. A super-sized duffel bag.
b. A medium-size purse.
c. A mini clutch.

4. The paparazzi are waiting outside the drugstore to snap your pic. What do you do before leaving the store?
a. Hit the makeup aisle and feverishly redo your face using all the testers.
b. Slip on your shades and reapply your gloss.
c. Nothing, just head out, smile, and wave!

5. You snooze through your alarm the morning of a job interview. Do you make it on time?
a. No way—it takes time to look good!
b. Yes, but you had to do your hair en route.
c. Sure, you arrive bare-faced and early!

TURN THE PAGE TO SEE YOUR RESULTS

mostly a's: you're diva-licious

Roll out the red carpet and grab that tiara—you're definitely in the running for the title of Queen Diva! Only your pillow knows what you look like when you first wake up and you'd never dream of leaving the house (gasp!) sans makeup. Just try to dial down the Diva every once in a while—even supermodels take days off!

mostly b's: you're a d.i.t. (diva-in-training!)

While running out of mascara wouldn't be your worst nightmare, you love to experiment with makeup and you like looking good. But you also know that there's a time and place to obsess over your hair and face. You may spend a lot of time getting ready for a big date, but you're also comfortable toning it down for, say, a game of ultimate Frisbee in the park!

mostly c's: you're the anti-diva

For you, diva is a four-letter word! You're a no-muss, no-fuss type of girl—a ponytail, a dab of mascara and a pinch of blush, and you're good to go. You'd much rather sleep in than spend loads of time in front of the mirror. Your fresh, natural, and never overdone look is the perfect match for your carefree, laid-back attitude.

WHICH WHITE HOUSE JOB ARE YOU DESTINED FOR?

Find out if you'll be hanging out in the Oval Office or somewhere else on the Hill!

1. Which one of these skills would make you a good detective? You:
a. Always create a plan of action.
b. Aren't afraid to confront and overcome obstacles.
c. Ask the right questions.

2. In kindergarten, you were known as the one who:
a. Wanted to be Simon in Simon Says.
b. Showed the other kids how to share.
c. Hogged Show and Tell time.

3. The prom queen vote is between you and your best friend. What do you do?
a. Run a tough but fair campaign.
b. Negotiate a deal to share the crown.
c. Talk up your friend but secretly hope to win.

4. When it comes to parties, you're the one who:
a. Insists on hosting them.
b. Make sure they don't get out of control.
c. Spreads the word via Facebook.

5. A girl at school is spreading rumors about your friends. What do you do?
a. Stand up for your friends.
b. Confront the girl right away and get her to stop.
c. Clear things up on your blog.

TURN THE PAGE TO SEE YOUR RESULTS

SCORING

mostly a's: president

People can sense that you're a natural-born leader, and
they know they can count on your master reasoning skills
to conquer any challenge. Your confidence shines through
in whatever you do. Better start practicing your State of the
Union voice—there could be a real West Wing in your future!

mostly b's: secretary of state

Being in the spotlight isn't as important to you as making
sure everything goes smoothly behind the scenes. You're
charming and responsible—you use your people skills to
sense when something's off and then you get right in there
to do damage control. As a result, people feel safe with you
and look to you for advice.

mostly c's: press secretary

You're a great communicator. Anything sounds interesting
when you're talking it up, whether it's a campaign to improve
school lunches or a movie you want to see. When you talk,
people don't just listen, they're convinced to act!

index